LOVEJOY ADRADOS

The Ultimate Debt Escape Plan

How to Completely Eliminate Your Debt for Good in Three Steps

First edition

This book was professionally typeset on Reedsy.
Find out more at reedsy.com

Debt is a shadow and can darken our path. But for the love of family, we find the strength to confront it, for love is our currency, and having a debt-free life is the key for our family's financial freedom.

LOVEJOY ADRADOS

Contents

1

Introduction

I was so confused and would not want to move on with my life. I am trapped.

That is exactly how I felt when I was deeply in debt. I never wanted to get out of bed. I do not want to check my bank account. I will have my coffee in the morning and all I can see are the bills piled up on my kitchen table I failed to open from the past few days. I felt like I have been burning out myself to work just to pay-off debts. The weight of the debts on my shoulders are like a constant shadow lurking in my daily life, whispering worries into my ears.

I kept on pretending that everything was fine. Until one day... it catches up with me. I feel so dumb and would never want to go on with my life. I felt so tired and confused on where to start and how to finish this mess.

Then one day, I realized, is this the kind of life I wanted for myself? For me to solve this problem, the best thing for me to do is to face it heads on. As much as I wanted to bury my head in the sand and pretend that my debts are not there, it can only stay hidden for so long.

Until I discovered the exact way on how to finally escape debt and use my cash flow to the fullest. Not only was I able to breathe easily on the payments, but I was able to save and invest full stop moving forward.

It's a rat race that I would never want to get back.

It's time that you also have the same result. Are you ready to say goodbye to debts for good? Let's go!

Why You Should Get Serious to Eliminate Your Debt

Do you want to have financial freedom? Free-up yourself from debt first. Debts restrict you to make a sound financial choice especially when they are taking major spaces in your brain. It is a heavy burden everyone wants to escape. Your most powerful wealth building tool is your income. By eliminating your debt, you will free up your significant portion of your income to build wealth. You will now have the flexibility to save, spend, or invest your money as you see fit. It will release you from the chains of slavery from your creditor that you have been holding back for a long time.

Do you want collecting agents to leave you alone for good? These calls are not giving you peace of mind at all. Constantly worrying about how to pay your debts and being afraid to take the call from the collecting agents is taking a toll on your mental health. By being debt-free, you will enjoy a greater peace of mind and as what we all wanted - will reduce your financial stress. You will finally be able to sleep soundly at night without worrying about how you are going to pay your debts. Isn't that an amazing feeling?

Also, debt payments can consume a significant portion of your monthly income. Imagine how much money you can free up when you eliminate your debt. This will allow you to enjoy a higher standard of living and you can now allocate your money towards achieving any financial goals that you have.

Most of the families who are in debt are also feeling the tension and financial stress inside and outside their homes. This stress can have a negative impact on your relationships with your loved ones. Being debt-free eliminates that stress and can lead to better communication at home.

If you want to retire with dignity, paying all of your debt will help you achieve it. Debt can be a major obstacle while saving your retirement. If you do not have payments, you can focus on allocating your money towards retirement instead. With this, the money you will put aside for your retirement will ensure a more comfortable and secure future for you and your family.

With all the benefits mentioned above, we can agree that by being serious about eliminating debt is a life-changing one. Being debt-free will reduce your stress, will build stronger relationships with your family, and will direct you into a more secure future. It also opens up your life into a world full of opportunities and most importantly, financial freedom.

To start this journey of being debt-free, all you have to do is to say "YES!" and follow the steps in this book. You will soon reap the benefits at the end and be amazed at the positive impact it can have on your life.

The Promise of a Debt-Free Future

Be ready to lose weight! Debts are like extra pounds that you drag with you everywhere. They are overbearing and will always be there if you're saddled with one. When you successfully pay off small debts, you will notice the weightlifting from your shoulders. You'll feel lighter and happier knowing that you're getting rid of this burden.

What's your status with debt? Do you have more than one loan? Are your balances increasing or decreasing each month? The answers to these questions are important.

The most important question, however, that you need to ask yourself is this: how did I get myself into this situation in the first place? The answer to that question is the key to your success. If you can answer this correctly then you'll know what went wrong and how to avoid it in the future. Once you know where you went wrong then it will be easier for you not to fall into the same traps ever again. If you had a lot of problems with managing money, then now is the time for a change.

When I started this journey, I was full of uncertainties and doubts. But I promise to myself that I will do my very best to make this happen for my family.

Same as with you, I will be your first supporter towards this journey. I would like to congratulate you in advance for taking a significant step towards transforming your financial life for the better. Being debt-free will turn into a distant-dream to an achievable reality.

Getting out of debt is not just about freeing up your finances but it's about liberating your life. Eliminating debt will open doors to new opportunities, lowering your stress level, and boosting your overall well-being.

But here's the deal. This book is not your fairy god mother who has a magic wand that can make your debts disappear. Instead, it's a road map that will help you to take control of your financial situation.

If you follow the instructions on this book, you are already 50% ahead of everyone else in life when it comes to money.

Doing this process will hurt you at some point because the reality will strike so bad that you do not want to be in that situation ever again. Your journey with this book might throw a curve ball or more, but with the proper guidance and with your determination, you will be debt-free – I promise.

2

Plan Your Debt Escape Plan

When it comes to getting out of debt, having a plan is essential. This is a plan that will help you guide your actions towards success. Without a plan, you won't know what to do next. A plan provides you with clarity and direction so you can walk confidently towards your goal.

A good plan will arm you with information and insights about your debt - how much it is, how it started, what problems it may cause and ways to solve it. Armed with this knowledge, you will be on a path towards debt resolution. If you can avoid securing debt altogether, that is even better. Without debt, you will be able to focus on other goals and have a life full of adventure and fun.

Speaking of adventure, have you ever been to an Escape Room? Imagine you are locked in and the clock is running out. To discover the key that unlocks the door, you must solve a variety of riddles and obstacles throughout the chamber. Your objective is to get away before time runs out.

Consider your bills as the obstacles in that room right now. Each debt requires a different challenge to be solved. It can be a vehicle loan, school loan, or credit card debt. Your debts stand in the way of your

5

ability to enjoy financial independence.

You only have a certain amount of time to deal with these debts, much as in the escape room. Each one grows more difficult the longer it takes to solve it. Interest begins to mount, making it even more difficult to get away.

The point is, you can team up with a proven financial method to defeat your debts just like you did with your team in the escape room. For instance, the debt snowball strategy resembles solving such problems one at a time. You start with the smallest debt and go to the biggest ones, gaining confidence and momentum along the way.

And it's like being debt-free when you eventually unlock that door and leave the escape room. You've overcome the obstacles, worked out the problems, and merited your financial independence.

Debt is not the end of the world - if you know how to eliminate it properly. Make your debt payoff plan a part of your monthly budget and pay more than what's required every time.

Thus, keep in mind that you have the ability to think, work as a team (with your financial plan), and beat the clock (interest rates) in order to escape the debt maze and achieve your financial goals, just like in an escape room.

It's Time to Keep the Debt Snowball Rolling!

The snowball analogy is a popular one because it's simple and it's easy to remember. But the truth is, we don't obtain the things that we want in life; we just keep on accumulating them. Debt is like a snowball as it grows bigger and bigger each day, taking us further away from our goals. Why build up a very small amount of debt when you can go all-in with everything you have?

When you have a debt problem, you need to reverse the avalanche.

That means reversing bad habits and changing your attitude towards money. Once you have cut down on your spending, start paying more than the minimum amount due. Start with paying off the small debts. Again, we're looking for quick wins.

Just like the Snowball, it will go bigger and bigger as it rolls down the hill. Meaning, you roll-over the amount of payment from your first small debt and use that to knock out the next smaller debt. By focusing on one debt, you will gain the momentum you need. You will be motivated to keep going, knowing that the victory is close at hand.

Why does this method work? This works because it changes your behavior about money. It changes the way you think about life and how you want to be in the future. You do not need any master's degree or any expertise to do this. All you need is your behavior!

Financial advisors advocate for paying off the largest debts first as you'll see a larger return on investment. But to be honest, I think this is a mistake.

There is this called Psychological Momentum. It changes your behavior and performance once you have accomplished something – big or small. Same as on paying off your debts, you acquire confidence and determination to take on bigger bills as you pay off each little one. It produces a positive feedback loop that gives your debt reduction efforts more traction.

With that, here's how this method works in three simple steps.

1. List all your debts from smallest to largest regardless of interest rate.
2. Attack your debts with gazelle intensity.
3. Cross the debt off once paid and move on to the next debt.Three simple steps, right? Yes, it's simple but it will give you challenges along the way but it will be worthy and rewarding at the end.

List Down Your Debts

The Debt Snowball method is a debt-reduction strategy. This method lets you pay your debts from smallest to largest. You gain your momentum by knocking out each of your debt. When the smallest balance of debt was paid, you apply that amount to the succeeding debt with the smaller amount making it faster for you to knock out every debt until you become debt free.

Why not just pay off the biggest one first? First, because it's not always possible. A lot of times, you need to take on more debt to pay off the ones you already have. The bigger the debt, the harder it is to pay it off. Therefore, you should start with small debts first and work your way up to larger loans.

How about the interest rate? Shouldn't I be paying for the debt that has a higher interest rate?

Forget about the interest rate when you do the Debt Snowball Method. If you started paying a car loan that is still four years outstanding with interest rate of 30%, you will see the number going down in balance but soon, you will get tired and lose morale that you will stop paying additional. Why was that? Because it's taking too long to get the win that you wanted while still dealing with your small debts.

If you ditch the smallest debt first, you can see the progress quickly! This will make you feel excited about knocking off your succeeding debts even more until you become debt-free. This also gives you the validation that this method works and that you can really make it happen.

This is why you should pay off small debts and work your way up to big ones. Eliminating small debts first will give you a sense of accomplishment and encourage you to continue your efforts and become debt free even faster! Imagine taking out the biggest debt first. Your morale is certainly low at one point, and you will stop thriving.

This could potentially snowball into other areas of your life. Forget about your credit score. This will only put you into more debts. So, paying off small debts first is a winning combination! The bottom line is that it is easier to become wealthy if you do not have any debt.

Face Your Biggest Enemy

Your goal is to have a large amount of money available that you can do whatever you like with - and that's called being wealthy. To become wealthy, the easiest way is for you not to have any debt payments. When it comes to debt, the best way for you not to have any of it is by not having any in the first place!

Get Ready to Take on the Enemy. Be prepared for this war. If you want to win this battle, then you need to have the right equipment.

You will need something that will help you win over your debts and keep them at bay. What kind of weapon should you have? You need a plan!

A typical American who earns $50,000 per year or around $4,200 per month would normally receive a net of tax of $3,125. On an average, an American will have $400 or more in monthly car payments, $1,200 or more in mortgage, and outstanding credit card debt of $200.

Here is the common type of debts that many American may have right now:

1. **Auto loan** - Purchasing a car would either require a down payment or not. No down payment means that you can purchase a car without upfront money but will result in higher monthly payment. The common down payment on the other hand of a new car is around 20% of the car's purchase price. For a $40,000 car, this will be an $8,000 down payment. The remaining balance will be paid via installment usually in a term of 3-6 years.

Technically, during the time of your loan contract, you are not the owner of either your car or your house. See that the Certificate of Registration of your car was named after the bank or the company you owe it with?

What will happen if at a certain time, the debtor defaulted on payment of the loan due to emergency reasons, and he does not have an emergency fund in place? He risks towing his car to the bank or will be forced to sell it.

2. **Mortgage Debt** - For mortgage payment, the average monthly payment in the USA can vary widely depending on its size, interest rate, and geographic location. On an average, Americans paid between around $1,500 per month on mortgage with loan tenure up to 30 years. Same with car loans, when you default on payment for a certain time, your house will be repossessed by the bank you owe it. Imagine how painful it will be for your family.

3. **Student loan** - One of the most acquired loans in the United States. These loans are offered by the federal government and private lenders, with varying terms and conditions. On Average, American students who graduated with bachelor's degrees can have $30,000 in student loan debt. Repayment period is standard 10 years but may be extended typically to 20 or 25 years. Using the standard 10 years tenure loan, monthly payments on an average will be $304. The payments will depend on the amount of the loan and interest rate.

However, while these student loans can provide access to education, it can also become a financial burden to the students once they graduate. You would like to graduate so you can start a new life but bringing a student loan with you will not give you a head-start in life. There is a potential to accumulate interest over the period of the loan and this will result in the borrower paying back significantly more than they initially owned. Do not fall into this trap.

4. **Credit Card Debt** - What about for the credit card payments? According to the Federal Reserve Bank of St. Louis, as of 2023, the number of card holders getting delinquent hit almost the same spot during COVID pandemic. People are losing their jobs; businesses are closing down. Technically, people are losing their sources of livelihood which makes them pay their credit cards in full.

People argue that credit cards can offer convenience. However, credit cards can make it easier for someone to overspend because it provides a source of readily available debt. Also, relying solely on credit cards for your spending can create psychological detachment. According to studies, it was shown that people tend to spend more when using their credit cards because they don't feel that the money is getting out of their pockets.

Some also argue that credit cards help them earn miles, points, and cash back. But these points will not make you rich. Not a single wealthy person will say that they earned their wealth by earning credit card points.

What's the deal if I pay them regularly anyway? Here's the deal. About 48% of credit card owners carried a balance at least in the past 12 months. Credit card average interest rates were at 22.16%.

Banks made a whopping $106 billion from credit card fees and interests.

Listen, the odds are not always in your favor. As a matter of fact, most people will miss payment once an emergency happens to them. Credit card interests are no joke either. Before you knew it, you were already deep in debt.

There is no way a person using a credit card can beat this system. Banks make it so admirable that credit cards are the most heavily advertised product out there. Even if you think you can make things work around the system, it's definitely not worth the risk.

5. **Medical Debt** – A trip to the hospital was never fun. Your kid got excited while riding his bike and accidentally fell on the road. Or maybe the basketball game became too physical, ending with a broken bone and a lot of crying.

   For whatever reason, one thing is for sure – nobody wanted to rack up those medical bills. Medical debt is overwhelming and nobody wants to be in that position especially if you do not have enough cash to wipe up the bills. Take a deep breath – you can do this and it's going to be okay.

The fastest way to build your wealth is to be debt free. While you are holding most of your personal things acquired through debt, you cannot be free financially if you are still in prison from all your credit.

With a monthly salary of $4,200, you can save and invest approximately $500 without any loan or debts. All you have to do is to secure your food, clothing, utilities, insurance, and other relevant expenses. If you do it in 10 to 15 years, you will no longer have to worry about your retirement and your future.

Now that you are convinced that you can be wealthy if you could get out of debt. The problem also is that you do not know how to get out of debt. You are finding a way on how to get free from it. I have good news for you! I have the sure-fire, but challenging method of getting yourself out of debt. But I tell you now, not all people are willing to do this because they find it difficult. That is why they are still in debt. But not you - you are different! You decided that you would like to live like no one else. That is why you will do this method.

For Step 1, list down your debt from smallest to highest. Okay, you might feel like it is the last thing you want to do at this moment, but this is exactly the first thing that you should do. Be honest to yourself and get real! No more sugar-coating. Get your pen and paper and write down all your debts from smallest to highest.

RANK	DEBT	REMAINING DEBT	MINIMUM PAYMENT
1	Mastercard	2,000	200
2	Visa Card	3,000	250
3	Hospital Bill	4,800	400
4	Car	20,160	420
5	Student loan	32,832	304
	TOTAL	**62,792**	**1,574**

Table 1. Illustration on how to list down your debts from smallest to largest

3

Attack the Debts

I n Nat Geo, we see gazelles outrun cheetahs time after time. Gazelles are lightly built, have long legs, and a small head. They can reach speeds of 60 miles an hour to outrun their predators. How do they do this? They focus 100% on outrunning the cheetah. They don't look at the trees, the grass, or even if they should take their left or right turn. Cheetah runs to get food, but gazelle runs for its life.

Imagine that debt is a cheetah running after you like a gazelle in the woods. High interest rates, escalating debt, and restless nights are all signs of that cheetah's relentlessness. The trick is that gazelles are intelligent and laser-focused, which allows them to survive. They try to outmaneuver the cheetah rather than out sprint it. Gazelle intensity is all about having a quick, unwavering concentration on your financial objectives.

By being a gazelle, you will be smart enough that your life depends on what you do today. Gazelle's primary hunter is the cheetah - the fastest animal in the land yet gazelle wins almost each time. Like in debt, your goal is to outmaneuver the enemy and run for your life to get out of debt.

For Step 2, attack the smallest debts by paying as much as you

possibly can. Once you have paid one debt, roll-over the money that you were paying from the first debt and add it as a payment to the next debt. That is why you called it Debt Snowball. The snowball gets bigger as it picks up more snow on the way.

But, how can I start rolling-over if I do not have the money to start over it?

Here, my friend, are the things that you should do to make it happen. Remember, you are a Gazelle, so be ready for this.

1. **<u>Cut the fat</u>** - Get into the budget and trip those fat! Gazelle focus entails eliminating those unnecessary expenses from your spending plan. It's not depriving yourself but putting a name on every penny. Really, do you need that daily cappuccino or all those clothing you seldom wear? Every dollar you save may be used to pay down your debt snowball. Making those difficult decisions today will enable you to experience financial independence tomorrow.

   These expenses might include cable, eating out, buying expensive clothing and shoes, or anything else that is not necessary for daily survival purposes. This could be a ruthless move but it's one that works! Just like before, the idea here is to focus 100% on getting rid of your debt - not the other stuff. You don't need to cut every expense, but you do need to take drastic measures to get rid of debt. You cannot do all of these if you do not have a budget.

   "Cutting the Fat" underlines the importance of being mindful of your spending, making conscious choices, and understanding that by prioritizing your financial goals and making small adjustments, you can achieve a debt-free, more secure future.

Once you have identified which part of your current expenses you can cut down, use that money to accelerate your payment on the smallest debt. In this sense, you will be paying more than what is required for you to pay for your debt.

Download a budgeting app, create a budgeting worksheet, or have a dedicated notebook that you can use for your budget. In whatever form that is, do it, as long as it is serving your purpose.

2. **Sell something you own** - Focus 100% on knocking off that debt with the snowball. Nothing else is important right now. So here comes garage sales!

You'll have to take radical measures, like selling your smartphone, to knock off every debt in your list. It may feel like the only way to get out of debt, but it is the right way.

Let's face it, most of us have a sizable collection of items we no longer require. There might be a ton of sporting goods, antique furniture, old kids' toys, or electronics in your garage that you were completely unaware of. There will be a treasure hunt soon.

That outdated bicycle lying around? There could be a happy buyer out there. That collection of old vinyl records? It sounds wonderful to a collector. Selling your possessions allows you to earn income rather than merely clearing out clutter.

Had a yard sale before? It's fun! It's like a huge goodbye tour for your goods. As more people arrive and make purchases, your debt decreases. Making money is important, but so is actively managing your finances.

You don't even need a yard in the modern world. The online market is on your side. Selling anything—from vintage toys to used electronics—is simple thanks to websites and apps. Someone else's treasure might be buried in your junk.

Selling your things could need some work, but consider it a further step in the direction of your debt-free objective. Realizing that your financial independence, rather than your possessions, may determine who you are is important. So, give up what you no longer need and watch your debt go more quickly than you ever imagined. You own it today, and you'll be financially free tomorrow.

3. **Stay laser-focus and cut those credit cards** - This method will work only if you stop accumulating more debt. Do not fool yourself by doing the Debt Snowball and still would like to use your credit card purchase more since you are saving money to pay off your debt.

Just as gazelles don't waste energy on things that won't help them live, you shouldn't spend your hard-earned money on things that won't help you pay off your debts. Gazelles don't get sidetracked by extravagant goods, and neither should you. Shiny things like a brand-new technology, a fancy automobile, or that unbelievable vacation offer could attract your attention, but they might derail your plans.

Forget about impulsive purchases and flashy credit card offers; both may quickly devastate your money. Impulsive expenditures and credit card offers that promise the moon can ruin your finances. You may get drawn in and find it more difficult to escape. Therefore, disregard them. They are not your traveling companions.

What is the best way to get yourself away from having to spend on things you do not need? Cut your credit cards! I have a strong stance against credit cards due to the risk of overspending. There is an emotional component when using a credit card. The ease of swiping a card makes it simpler to go over budget and overspend. Because credit cards don't seem like real money, people tend to spend more with them than they would with cash.

Are you trying to keep the points for future airline miles? Here's the thing, nobody gets rich by earning airline miles. It's the banks who own skyscrapers and sports arenas, not you. When you use your credit card, it exposes you to a lot of risk. You cannot win the game on this credit card game and the best way to win is not to play this game.

4. **Get part time jobs** - If you've tried everything else, and you still have a balance on one of your debts, consider getting a part-time job. I'm not talking about leaving your job for another one and losing the income. I mean working an extra hour or two a day for cash. You can do this while still going to school or working full time. If you are in over your head with credit card debt, this may be the only way to get rid of that debt without selling your stuff or taking money from family members.

Do not mind what other people are telling you. People who are wealthy do not mind what other people think about them. You have to live like no one else so later you can be someone else.

If you've done everything in your power to knock down your debts, and you are still stuck with some left over, consider getting a second job. Just like before, this is something that you do just for cash. You don't need the money except to pay your debt. So, you focus 100% on the debt and nothing else.

I won't be getting into what exactly it is you can do to get around your first job, but I will say that there are a few things you can do to get extra cash. They are bartering some items at yard sales; selling items on eBay; and getting a part-time job so you can lessen your debt. All these things will help you in the long run.

5. **Celebrate small wins** - Yeah, doing this step might make you feel bored at first. But remember that each debt you pay off is a victory, no matter the size. Imagine climbing a mountain. You don't just celebrate when you reach the peak; you celebrate every step you take upward. The same goes for your debt-free journey. Whether you've paid off a massive loan or a tiny credit card balance, it's a win. It means you're making progress, and that's something to cheer for.

Every time you cross out a debt, treat yourself within reason. Celebrations don't have to break the bank. It could be a simple pleasure—a movie night at home, a favorite dessert, or a relaxing bath. The key is to acknowledge your hard work and perseverance. By rewarding yourself, you reinforce the positive behavior of managing your finances wisely. Besides, who never wanted to have those relaxation times after a great job crossing out a debt?

Most importantly, use these celebrations to fuel your determination towards achieving your objective. Celebrating small wins isn't just about feeling good in the moment. It's about motivation.

When you mark these milestones, it boosts your confidence and determination. It's like a shot of adrenaline that keeps you charging ahead.

Here are some of the simple and down-to-earth small-win celebrations you can do that will cost you little to no money.

- *Cook a Special Meal at Home*: Make a handmade, gourmet meal for you and your loved ones. Make your favorite food or try a new recipe, then enjoy it together. Not only will the family love it but the bond together will be amazing.
- *Movie Night In*: Set up a comfortable movie night at home with snacks and your preferred movies or TV shows. It's a cost-effective substitute for going to the movies.
- *Take a Soothing Bath*: Light some candles, run a warm bath, and unwind. For an additional touch of relaxation, add some calming music or a nice book.
- *Outdoor adventure*: Arrange a picnic at a local park, a bike trip, or a stroll in the forest. Spend time outside taking in the fresh air and the beauty of nature.

When you focus, the debt snowball splinters. It might take a while to build the snowball back up again. But, if you focus on the debt, it will get smaller and smaller. When it gets small enough, you can throw it away. By focusing on one debt at a time you will gain momentum. You'll be motivated to keep going, knowing that the victory is close at hand.

4

Keep it Rolling, Baby!

The obedient you listed your debts lined up from smallest to largest. You've trimmed the fat from your budget and embraced gazelle intensity. Now, it's time to dive into the heart of the debt snowball method – paying off that very first debt.

Paying-off your first debt will be a huge step for you. This part is the most challenging yet rewarding part. For this first time ever, you now know how to strike off your debts for good.

The power of the first payment now begins. **For Step 3, pay the first debt and roll-over the money**. Take that extra money that you have freed up from step number two and channel it like a laser onto the smallest debt. Do not be emotional about changing your list. The smallest debt should be your target. This time, you are not only making minimum payments but also throwing on that extra money that you had on your smallest debt. It might feel like a small pebble at the foot of a mountain, but remember, every avalanche starts with a single snowflake.

Now, show that debt who is the boss. Once you've made that final payment, there's a moment of sheer triumph. You cross that debt off your list, and it's a victory parade in your financial world. It might be small, but it's yours, and who cares? Here is where the snowball gets even cooler – for the next round of payment, you take the money that you used when paying the first debt and roll it onto the next one.

This is where the snowball kicks in. With the money that you are paying on the first small debt plus the amount of minimum payment you are making on the second one, you attack the next debt with even more force. Now your snowball increases as it rolls down the hill, getting bigger and faster as it goes. Your debt buster progress accelerates, and you start to see those debts disappearing faster than you thought possible. It's a powerful feeling, and it's all thanks to that first payment and the debt snowball method.

The Debt Snowball Illustration

Let us have a real-life scenario for you to easily learn the Debt Snowball method. Let's say you have the following six debts. You have arranged them based on the smallest to the biggest amount of outstanding balance as of this day.

RANK	DEBT	REMAINING DEBT	MINIMUM PAYMENT
1	Mastercard	2,000	200
2	Visa Card	3,000	250
3	Hospital Bill	4,800	400
4	Car	20,160	420
5	Student loan	32,832	304
	TOTAL	**62,792**	**1,574**

Table 2. List of debts with minimum payments

You have a credit card outstanding balance with MasterCard and Visa amounting to $2,000 and $3,000, respectively. You also have a hospital bill with a remaining balance of $4,800 on which you pay at least

$400 monthly. You bought a car two years ago with a remaining loan amount of $20,160. You thought you could not go to college without a payment. That's why you applied for a loan with an outstanding balance of $32,832.

Let's see how long originally it will take you to eliminate your listed debt assuming you will not do the Debt Snowball Method.

RANK	DEBT	REMAINING DEBT	MINIMUM PAYMENT	MONTHS TO BE PAID
1	Mastercard	2,000	200	10
2	Visa Card	3,000	250	12
3	Hospital Bill	4,800	400	12
4	Car	20,160	420	48
5	Student loan	32,832	304	108
	TOTAL	62,792	1,574	

Table 3. List of debts with minimum payments and number of months to knock them off without Debt Snowball Method

Using the Debt Snowball Method, pay all minimum amounts due to all debts except for the smallest debt. Since you are very determined and super focused to get out of debt, you decided to get an additional side-hustle which will bring you an additional $350 per month. This could also be from expenses minimized monthly. New payment of $550 for debt number 1 ($200 minimum payment + $350 side hustle). Total new payment with the Debt Snowball Method is now $1,924 per month.

To knock out the $2,000 MasterCard Credit Card, pay the additional $350 on top of your monthly payment of $200. The debt is completely gone in four months which originally should be 10 months because of the Snowball Method. The difference of $200 on the fourth month will now be applied as additional payment to your Visa Credit Card. Instead of paying only $250, you will now pay $450 in the first month leaving an outstanding balance of $1,800 for Visa Credit Card.

		Mastercard	Visa Card
Remaining amount of debt		2,000	3,000
Minimum payments		200	250
DEBT SNOWBALL METHOD			
Month1	Minimum payment	200	250
	Side Hustle	350	350
Month2	Minimum payment	200	250
	Side Hustle	350	350
Month3	Minimum payment	200	250
	Side Hustle	350	350
Month4	Minimum payment	200	250
	Side Hustle	350	150	200
Total payment		2,000	1,200
Remaining balance		-	1,800

Table 4. Completely knock-off first debt in four months

Now you have knocked out your MasterCard Credit Card debt, crossed it out and rolled over the amount you are paying from it to second debt. Total new payment for the Visa Card will now be $800. Do the same process to knock off debt number two, your Visa Credit Card.

RANK	DEBT	REMAINING DEBT	MINIMUM PAYMENT	NEW PAYMENT
1	~~Mastercard~~	-	-	-
2	Visa Card	3,000	250	800
3	Hospital Bill	4,800	400	400
4	Car	20,160	420	420
5	Student loan	32,832	304	304
	TOTAL	**60,792**	**1,374**	**1,924**

Table 5. Cross out first debt and calculate for the new payment of the second debt

As you have observed, you are gaining more and more funds for your debt payments. This is how the Debt Snowball works. As you roll, knocking out your debt, you will have more money to pay on the succeeding debts.

		Mastercard	Visa Card	Hospital Bill
Remaining amount of debt		2,000	3,000	4,800
Minimum payments		200	250	400
DEBT SNOWBALL METHOD				
Month 1	Minimum payment		200	250	400
	Side Hustle	350	350		
Month 2	Minimum payment		200	250	400
	Side Hustle	350	350		
Month 3	Minimum payment		200	250	400
	Side Hustle	350	350		
Month 4	Minimum payment		200	250	400
	Side Hustle	350	150	200	
Month 5	Minimum payment			250	400
	Previous payment for debt#1	200		200	
	Side Hustle	350		350	
Month 6	Minimum payment			250	400
	Previous payment for debt#1	200		200	
	Side Hustle	350		350	
Month 7	Minimum payment			200	400
	Previous payment for debt#1	200			200
	Previous payment for debt#2	50			50
	Side Hustle	350			350
Total payment		2,000	3,000	3,400
Remaining balance		-	-	1,400

Table 6. Completely knock-off second debt in seven months

In the 7th month, you will be able to pay off your second debt. Last payment will be only $200 and the remaining $50 will be applied to your Hospital Bill.

RANK	DEBT	REMAINING DEBT	MINIMUM PAYMENT	NEW PAYMENT
1	~~Mastercard~~			
2	~~Visa Card~~			
3	Hospital Bill	4,800	400	1,200
4	Car	20,160	420	420
5	Student loan	32,832	304	304
	TOTAL	**57,792**	**1,124**	**1,924**

Table 7. Cross out second debt and calculate for the new payment of third debt

Now you have knocked out your Visa Credit Card debt, crossed it out and rolled over the amount you are paying from it to the third debt. Total new payment for your hospital bill will now be $1,200. Do the same process to knock off the succeeding debt.

If you are consistent with the method, you will be able to knock out your hospital bill by the ninth month. Last payment in the ninth month for the hospital bill is $200. Use the remaining fund to roll over on the fourth debt, which is your car loan.

		Mastercard	Visa Card	Hospital Bill	Car
Remaining amount of debt		2,000	3,000	4,800	20,160
Minimum payments		200	250	400	420
DEBT SNOWBALL METHOD					
Month 1	Minimum payment		200	250	400	420
	Side Hustle	350	350		
Month 2	Minimum payment		200	250	400	420
	Side Hustle	350	350		
Month 3	Minimum payment		200	250	400	420
	Side Hustle	350	350		
Month 4	Minimum payment		200	250	400	420
	Side Hustle	350	150	200	
Month 5	Minimum payment			250	400	420
	Previous payment for debt#1	200		200	
	Side Hustle	350		350	
Month 6	Minimum payment			250	400	420
	Previous payment for debt#1	200		200	
	Side Hustle	350		350	
Month 7	Minimum payment			200	400	420
	Previous payment for debt#1	200			200	
	Previous payment for debt#2	50			50	
	Side Hustle	350			350	
Month 8	Minimum payment				400	420
	Previous payment for debt#1	200			200	
	Previous payment for debt#2	250			250	
	Side Hustle	350			350	
Month 9	Minimum payment				200	420
	Previous payment for debt#1	200				200
	Previous payment for debt#2	250				250
	Previous payment for debt#3	200				200
	Side Hustle	350				350
Total payment		2,000	3,000	4,800	4,780
Remaining balance		-	-	-	15,380

Table 8. Completely knock off debt in nine months

Cross out the hospital bill, and completely forget about it! Whew! You are already half-way and it was hard work already on your side. Congratulations. Do not forget to have a celebration every time you cross out any debt. This will help you have that sense of motivation to work towards the other debts.

RANK	DEBT	REMAINING DEBT	MINIMUM PAYMENT	NEW PAYMENT
1	~~Mastercard~~			
2	~~Visa Card~~			
3	~~Hospital Bill~~			
4	Car	20,160	420	1,620
5	Student loan	32,832	304	304
	TOTAL	52,992	724	1,924

Table 9. Cross out third debt and calculate for the new payment of fourth debt

You are now on your way to knock off two of your biggest debts. You are now going to pay $1,620 for your car loan. Imagine if you have another side hustle or other income source, you can add them up to your payments and will end your agony earlier. For now, let us stick to this example.

As you continue to be consistent with paying off the remainder of your car loan, you will be able to knock it off on the 19th month with some of the portion of your payment to be used to pay off the last debt which is the student loan debt. You may refer to the end part of the book for the entire illustration of the Debt Snowball Method.

Now, you can already cross out your car loan. No more burden of having your car pulled-out if you were not able to pay it. It's all yours now, enjoy!

RANK	DEBT	REMAINING DEBT	MINIMUM PAYMENT	NEW PAYMENT
1	~~Mastercard~~			
2	~~Visa Card~~			
3	~~Hospital Bill~~			
4	~~Car~~			
5	Student loan	32,832	304	1,924
	TOTAL	32,832	304	1,924

Table 10. Cross out car loan and use all the money to attack your last debt

All you have to do now is to pay the last debt that you have. Your student loan. After a year of hard work and dedication on this journey, this will be your last stretch so finish this strong as ever!

Continue paying your student loan debt and put whatever extra cash you have right now. Focus and put your gazelle-mindset forward. With your consistent effort, you will be able to pay off your student loan in 33rd month. Refer to the full illustration on the last part of this book.

Congratulations, fellow debt conqueror! You've unlocked the power of the debt snowball method without any fancy financial jargon or complicated formulas. Along the way, you've discovered that conquering debt isn't just about money but also requires determination and discipline. Every small win counts, and each success brings you closer to a life free from financial burdens.

RANK	DEBT	AMOUNT	MINIMUM PAYMENT	MONTHS TO BE PAID	DEBT SNOWBALL
1	Mastercard	2,000	200	10	4
2	Visa Card	3,000	250	12	7
3	Hospital Bill	4,800	400	12	9
4	Car	20,160	420	48	19
5	Student loan	32,832	304	108	33
	TOTAL	62,792	1,574		

Table 11. Comparison of number of months without and with Debt Snowball Method

It is also important to consider how many months you can reduce your debt with the Debt Snowball Method. Table 11 shows that you were able to fulfill your payments in 33 months, which is less than three years, as opposed to 108 months or nine long years.

Instead of stressing about your debt payments, you will now use the years you have saved to build your wealth. A huge relief!

Remember, it's not about how you start but the momentum you build. Like a snowball rolling down a hill, your progress accelerates with every debt you eliminate, and before you know it, that mountain of debt is gone.

Now that you're on the other side of your debt journey, you can breathe easy, walk tall, and enjoy financial freedom. No more monthly payments or stress weighing you down. You get to decide where your money goes. Invest more, save more, or treat yourself to that well-deserved vacation.

With your newfound financial freedom comes a world of possibilities. You can pursue work that fulfills you, take calculated risks, or pay it forward by helping others achieve financial freedom. It's essential to stay the course, keep budgeting, and continue building your wealth.

Your journey doesn't end here; it's just beginning. You have the skills, determination, and wisdom to thrive and define your financial future. Embrace your newfound freedom, and know that financial peace and endless opportunities await.

5

Conclusion

Hooray! Those pesky loan payments are now history! You've just finished a fantastic adventure—the climb to escape the debt trap. You've learned about the Debt Snowball Method, followed the instructions, and are now on the verge of financial freedom. But what comes after? Let's now dive into it.

First and foremost, pause to recognize your accomplishments. It takes a lot of effort to pay off debt, but you've done it! Every payment made—regardless of how little or large the debt—moved you closer to your financial objectives. Come on, you owe it to yourself for doing all the actions and hard work. There's only one thing that has to be done - let's celebrate! This time, you can take more than a small celebration. Level it up by having some nice dinner outside with your family, taking them to a paid movie, and other simple getaways (within reason).

You see, your road toward debt freedom doesn't end here. Financial freedom requires not just getting out of debt but also maintaining that debt-free status. It's important to keep up the discipline and spending practices you've developed along the way. Continue setting aside money for savings and wealth-building. Do not ever go back to those credit cards and debts again.

It's time to refocus your financial efforts on other objectives now that those monthly loan payments are no longer necessary. What aspirations have you been delaying? Create a plan to reach your new financial objectives, whether they are investing for retirement, saving for your kid's college education, buying a home, or saving for a dream vacation.

This discovered information shouldn't be kept to oneself. Share it with someone you know who might be dealing with debt. Support, advise, and inspire your friends and family. For someone else on their path to debt freedom, your experience might serve as a ray of hope.

Revel in the independence that comes with being debt-free. It's not just about having money, it's about having options and possibilities. The world is your oyster! So, take the reins of your financial future with confidence, knowing that you have the skills, determination, and smarts to succeed

6

References

These sources form the basis of the book and provide you with a trustworthy road map for taking on your debts and taking control of your financial future.

https://www.zippia.com/advice/average-american-income/

https://www.stlouisfed.org/publications/regional-economist/2023/aug/deja-vu-recent-rise-credit-card-debt-delinquencies

https://www.experian.com/blogs/ask-experian/state-of-credit-cards/

https://www.federalreserve.gov/releases/g19/hist/cc_hist_tc_levels.html

chrome-extension://efaidnbmnnnibpcajpcglclefindmkaj/https://www.federalreserve.gov/publications/files/2021-report-economic-well-being-us-households-202205.pdf

THE ULTIMATE DEBT ESCAPE PLAN

		Mastercard	Visa Card	Hospital Bill	Car	Student loan	Total
Remaining amount of debt		2,000	3,000	4,800	20,160	32,832	62,792
Minimum payments		200	250	400	420	304	1,574
DEBT SNOWBALL METHOD							
Month 1	Minimum payment		200	250	400	420	304	1,574
	Side Hustle	350	350					350
Month 2	Minimum payment		200	250	400	420	304	1,574
	Side Hustle	350	350					350
Month 3	Minimum payment		200	250	400	420	304	1,574
	Side Hustle	350	350					350
Month 4	Minimum payment		200	250	400	420	304	1,574
	Side Hustle	350	150	200				350
Month 5	Minimum payment			250	400	420	304	1,374
	Previous payment for debt#1	200		200				200
	Side Hustle	350		350				350
Month 6	Minimum payment			250	400	420	304	1,374
	Previous payment for debt#1	200		200				200
	Side Hustle	350		350				350
Month 7	Minimum payment			200	400	420	304	1,324
	Previous payment for debt#1	200			200			200
	Previous payment for debt#2	50			50			50
	Side Hustle	350			350			350
Month 8	Minimum payment				400	420	304	1,124
	Previous payment for debt#1	200			200			200
	Previous payment for debt#2	250			250			250
	Side Hustle	350			350			350
Month 9	Minimum payment				200	420	304	924
	Previous payment for debt#1	200			200			200
	Previous payment for debt#2	250			250			250
	Previous payment for debt#3	200			200			200
	Side Hustle	350			350			350
Month 10	Minimum payment					420	304	724
	Previous payment for debt#1	200				200		200
	Previous payment for debt#2	250				250		250
	Previous payment for debt#3	400				400		400
	Side Hustle	350				350		350
Month 11						1,620	304	1,924
Month 12						1,620	304	1,924
Month 13						1,620	304	1,924
Month 14						1,620	304	1,924
Month 15						1,620	304	1,924
Month 16						1,620	304	1,924
Month 17						1,620	304	1,924
Month 18						1,620	304	1,924
Month 19	Minimum payment					420	304	724
	Previous payment for debt#1	200				200		200
	Previous payment for debt#2	250				180	70	250
	Previous payment for debt#3	400					400	400
	Side Hustle	350					350	350
Month 20	Minimum payment						304	304
	Previous payment for debt#1	200					200	200
	Previous payment for debt#2	250					250	250
	Previous payment for debt#3	400					400	400
	Previous payment for debt#4	420					420	420
	Side Hustle	350					350	350
Month 21							1,924	1,924
Month 22							1,924	1,924
Month 23							1,924	1,924
Month 24							1,924	1,924
Month 25							1,924	1,924
Month 26							1,924	1,924
Month 27							1,924	1,924
Month 28							1,924	1,924
Month 29							1,924	1,924
Month 30							1,924	1,924
Month 31							1,924	1,924
Month 32							1,924	1,924
Month 33							1,224	1,224
Total payment		2,000	3,000	4,800	20,160	32,832	62,792
Remaining balance		-	-	-	-	-	-

Complete Debt Snowball Illustration

34

About the Author

Lovejoy, often known as LJ, has a Master of Business Administration and is a Certified Public Accountant. She is the creator of Savewithlove.com, a financial advocate, entrepreneur, writer, and mother to two incredible children. Her articles are geared on helping parents with household finances and budgeting.

You can connect with me on:
- https://bit.ly/LovejoyAdrados
- https://facebook.com/lovejoycpa

Subscribe to my newsletter:
- https://savewithlove.com/free-budget-tracker